| COURSE NUMBER | SUBJECT | EXAM | TYPE | FINAL GRADE |
|---|---|---|---|---|
| 1724 | ENGLISH 7 | 72 | | 70 |
| 2724 | SOC ST 7 | 63 | | 54 |
| 3724 | IMAGERY | 52 | | 60 |
| 4724 | TROPE | 62 | | 67 |
| 5050 | SELF-REGULATION | 70 | | 74 |
| 5060 | BLISS | 51 | | 55 |
| 5070 | RESPONSIBILITY | 48 | | 49 |
| 5080 | IFL/GERMAN | 67 | | 62 |
| 8010 | METONYMY | 65 | | 68 |
| 8210 | HEALTH | 57 | | 54 |
| 8410 | ART 7 | 55 | | 50 |
| 8770 | MIXED CHORUS | 32 | | 44 |
| 8910 | METRE | 50 | | 53 |
| 9900 | PE 7 BOYS | 53 | | 51 |

# JON PAUL FIORENTINO NEEDS IMPROVEMENT

COACH HOUSE BOOKS | TORONTO

first edition

  Canadä

Published with the generous assistance of the Canada Council for the Arts and the Ontario Arts Council. Coach House also acknowledges the support of the Government of Canada through the Canada Book Fund and the Government of Ontario through the Ontario Book Publishing Tax Credit.

LIBRARY AND ARCHIVES CANADA CATALOGUING IN PUBLICATION

Fiorentino, Jon Paul
    Needs Improvement / Jon Paul Fiorentino – First edition.

Poems.
Issued in print and electronic formats.
ISBN 978 1 55245 280 6 (pbk) – ISBN 978 1 77056 357 5 (epub)

    I. Title.

PS8561.I585N43 2013          C811'.6          C2013-904096-X

Purchase of the print version of this book entitles you to a free digital copy. To claim your ebook of this title, please email sales@chbooks.com with proof of purchase or visit chbooks.com/digital. (Coach House Books reserves the right to terminate the free digital download offer at any time.)

*Neither the Austinian promise nor the Althusserian prayer require a pre-existing mental state to 'perform' in the way that they do.*

— Judith Butler

*Dedicated to the memory of Robert Kroetsch*

# THINGS-AS-FACTS

ALYRICS

## THINGS-AS-FACTS

The flesh-splashed summer risk
the long-glare congestion guarantee
the inadequacy of the what-you-knows
the unwelcome breeze, the calming allergens

There are parks and buildings and transport
and then there's your tacit asyndeton:
you remove, you revise, you mute
you want to tell me things you never will

First, you had it in your mind to construct
a rubric, a gift, a translation tool
that would allow us to present things-as-facts
you couldn't find the language

But, with your latest, defeatist polysyndeton,
you found a way to dream
and design and compose
the most pressing need for it

In ill Nauset I messaged you
in old Montreal I invoked you
in dead Winnipeg I owned you
I am wrong again

You should heed the words
of your last, last manager
(whatever those were)

In dreary Vancouver I exorcised you
in ruddy Brooklyn I remade you
in perfect Winnipeg I rewrote you
I am wrong again

## LOWERHAND

String prose units, inversions
all the way to rural

Find ways to unthread then stitch up then
consummate lexical decoration then trash it

Your sleeve, your heart, your sleep, your spleen

Prepare existential theses *in medias res*
or support local load-bearing relics

Let the winter do its kind work so
steal an almost-vintage jacket

Your layers, your work, your laugh, your use

Ensure your phrases enforce
tenets of exuberance

Don't alter a thing
gain the lowerhand

Your head, your case, your tense
            you're strong

How is your daughter?

Do you still
live in Wolseley?

Do you still
have some issues?

Did they give
you that settlement?

Did it pay off
your mortgage?

Are you still
unemployed?

Are you still
unemployable?

She writes:

*I've never had imposter syndrome*
*because everyone has always had it for me.*

*And whenever anyone says, 'I love you,'*
*I say, 'No, you are.'*

A file break undertow
wishes coma parallel

Phone call collection
agent misery and mulch

Brine dreg cellophane
never-hooded suicide on hold

Common paraplectic sorry
ruin and rune comma apology

I'm too old it happens
it happens

## MINIMAL PAIR: SIMPLETONS

When I said we made a minimal pair
I was deep in linguistic conceit

It had nothing to do with your character
it was strictly labio-dental

189 Allenby Crescent –
swollen breath, gravel
chase me back there, boys

Or recess –
hide under the large slide, descend
above me, girls

Eight-track stereo –
croon Dylan's Christianest album
all shag-carpet orchestral

Some basement –
pucks shot with splintered sticks
battered washer/dryer

Vocational high school –
chase Father's white rum with Mother's
diet soda

The perfectly good air –
choke on it
settle for being the perfectly bad son

Now –
the long slide,
the trickle-down dying

When we hate to have been excited by Winnipeg, what kind of hate do we make? We ascribe an agency to Winnipeg, a power to excite, and position ourselves as the objects of its excitable geography. We hate that Winnipeg acts, and acts against us, and the hate we make is a further instance of Winnipeg, one that seeks to arrest the metonymy of the prior placing. Thus, we exercise the metonymy of Winnipeg even as we seek to counter its metonymy, caught up in a bind that no act of storage can undo.

The title of 'The Winnipeg Cold Storage Company' poses the question of collective memory and what it means to say that 'things might be done with storage.' The problem of collective memory is thus immediately bound up with a question of performance. What does it mean for storage not only to store, but also in some sense to perform and, in particular, to perform what it stores?

Recent proposals to regulate Winnipeg myth on site, in the facility, and in other similar facilities, have spawned a set of ambivalent cultural consequences. The spectre of regionalism has become a privileged haunting in which to re-evaluate the cause and effects of civic shame.

The question of whether citizenship requires the repression of Winnipeg is not new, but the recent efforts to regulate the self-storage of citizenship within Winnipeg repose this question in a different light. After all, Winnipeggers enjoy some of the rights and obligations of citizenship, but not all of them.

To argue that certain archives of Winnipeg are more properly construed as identity rather than history sidesteps the question of storage. Storage now appears to be the repression of citizenship, and if Winnipeg or pornography or the mayor's office or cold are no longer accepted as 'history' then the repression of any of those customs would no longer appear to be Winnipeg.

Down to my last
lyric

Do you know the word *pilling*?
It's a piling on of fabrications

You wear it well or
wore it

Free-range derangement commences
as denizens make strange with tenses and moods

I saw an old cancerous friend here
who said, 'I remember when I used to be creative –

They cut it out of me
all interstitial-like'

Now, the lies and years are
piling/pilling

I will miss you when you shun me. I write these
things for nothing

You remain
the best nothing I know

With decades behind, one still boorishly chases the dull candles held by those somehow traipsing through the uncomplicated life; one just an acknowledgements page away from calling it now, one page away from done. Over it. So very over it. With a brisk rendering of complexity, shrill and shrugged repeats of days, and one is an unparented swiller and one's tonic and balm no longer enough. Soon there will be no verb. The countables wreck their own units; static laughs, lit up and tweak-weary. Diplomacy taints the micropolitic. Countless hours, of course, spark sluggish decades and one loses games one isn't even aware of. There is this one thing that all things are made of, one says, and the dull-witted say, 'yes, this.' One does not, should not. Still rhetoric eases. The peculiar sting of fact-unchecked quirk-factor hymnals and yet one chases slow-moving candles and one fattens and withers in season – slow metronome. A slow, stupid metronome. Then, at some point, there is no real verb but an unrelenting need to call it and to call it in time, listlessly, to call one's own over it.

Write of the solitary fence post
of the day you heard the incantatory wisdom of birds of Alberta
and how the peculiar birdsong of the tundra swan once set your
spirit free

Write of the struggles of your fathers
of the linguistic imperatives that shackle you and keep you from
articulating the particularities of non-heteronormative and
alternative identities

Write of the land and how it's shaped you
of the small things like the footsteps you hear when you wish
to hear nothing and the incomprehensible strangeness of being
and exactly what you have gleaned

Write of the day that you lost her
of the day that you lost him and everything collapsed into
emblems and metaphors and similes and other tropes blending
into the cruellest and sharpest unit of metonomy

Write of the city that you left there
of the Winnipeg half-jokes, the myth-making memos, the spray
paint and solvents, the cult of new money, the rebuild and let-
down, the angst of personae, the collective of lonely

Let jargon
let twinning

Find frail ones
find, kill them

Execute without extremities
execute with outsourcing

Precision in the playlist
precision – the oldest dreck in the book

Couplets are unkind
couplets

COME BACK

No such thing as comebacks. Treacle
soon-to-be

When that happens
you will know the reasons

Because the reasons are the things —
mistakes, sight gags, people you've hurt

Now on a loop ordered from least
to most malignant

A score. Let's just
call it that when it begins again

The most impressive diarist —
such a meagre diary

One million documentaries
such unkind documentation

A torrent of confessionals —
a gush and the land is yours

Infinite eulogies
you know the elective logic here —

You made it and
you slay it every time

If you bandy about protocols for the dance card; it is okay and it's ok to speak in clear sentences even though there isn't a dance (there never will be)

You may propose and propose. Let us be clear and let's be precise. Your purpose of things is borne out of exalted forecasts, broadcasts

The broadcasts diminish in real time as we diminish slightly faster. It is okay to speak in clear sentences and it's ok to say a thing before the broadcast's end

It is sooner than you applied for. The quickened wretched hubris calms you – an HDMI swaddling. The thing is, it is okay. It's ok to speak in a clear sentence or to even

Risk more than one. It is okay and it's ok to not let the terrible, accurate tune pass you by; it is okay and it's ok to feel alone and Dopplered. That is what it does and that's what

Totally okay to have lost it in the process of nothing other than losing. Totally and it is okay. It's ok. I promise. Although these things called promises never quite exist. I promise

This testament seems perfect
so perfect so right – is it new?

So obvious entirely oblivious that our
distance is orchestral, choleric

You're in rim-shot pratfall proximity
control this sanguine scatter

Suck the chloroform choir dry –
revisionist hymnal tablets touch

The song lies and you knew it
but that's the thing about aging –

Some songs might

Because poetry is very, very far from –
and those who therefore thrive insist it remain so

And also contemplative drones drone
inside cabalist cocooneries

Not to mention domain names reserved for only the most
wicked eloquent –

Plus flaccid fraternities with their
heightened-flaccidity-as-aesthetic-mandate flail, swing

Most meritorious solder wand weld torch trophy crooners
croon the comments, the walls, avoid the wells

And wasn't this ambition supposed to be in the writing, not in its
product? In tenor and vehicle and not in laurel and mantle?

Fuck me. I'm as flail as anyone

All love is careless
bleating sadly into some thing or other or
mainlining its way into varicose

The millionaires of summer
swelter away in Old Montreal
delve deep into marry me's

I'm scared all the way
down the skill hull
it's always a point of almost-pride

No setting to this poem
but your mind's all right
and the pediatricians are sleeping
so just skulk softly

Live stream

Nothing here
but anchors

Home never lasts, outlasts
there are windows walls ceilings
broken bottles respirator floors
dialysis terrace instant messaging
machines and mescaline fails

I've been alone and I like it –
collectivity of nouns running
vacant – city hall unencumbered
one incumbent in the mix splitting
sides taking names for day surgery

It's never felt more like
homing beacon dirge drop the shadows
on the porcelain orange surge the long
way make it stick pray to something smaller
than myself go to hell make it humour

GAG

Entirely my idea
not a great one but entirely mine

There was a bicycle and an objectivist poet
sort of riding it

Not red or blue
entirely my idea all twig and spoke and gag

I gag often these days like as if it wouldn't catch up
never my bicycle always entirely my idea

And I share the poet with a post-mountain
time scholar from out east

Grey
not silver but entirely grey

There is a mostly red, cylindrical ashtray. Right there. On a picnic table. Concentrate. It is mostly empty. You will notice there is one half-smoked cigarette in it. A Viceroy. The red ashtray on the picnic table is in the park and so are you.

Does the ashtray belong to someone? No. It did but it doesn't. What kind of red is it? You don't know the name for it yet. It's similar to what's left of the red on your nails. You tell yourself Pantone 185C. It is Pantone 185C.

Do you want it? You do but you don't. You don't smoke anymore but you want to. Cylindrical Pantone 185C appeals. Why did someone bring and leave Pantone 185C in the park? What was that someone thinking? Your first thought is he wasn't thinking.

But if he was, what was he thinking? Did he think it was too precise? An emblem of a person he no longer wants to see in emblems? Someone who had hurt him? He doesn't like to be hurt. So he brought it and left it. Emblems, in poems as in parks, are boring.

You know this. Why are you drawn to it? You are drawn to it because you look up and there are old women, young women, old men, young men, children, whole families, half-families in the park. They all wear little squares of Pantone 185C.

# NEEDS IMPROVEMENT

PEDAGOGICAL INTERVENTIONS

1 Shut the door. Lock the door. Wash the students.

2 Ensure that kindling from previous exams is removed.

3 Any scrap of confidence, kindness, goodwill, etc., MUST be removed.

4 Arrange the desks in a panopticonic manner. In the middle, fashion a watchtower out of chairs, Saran Wrap and duct tape.

5 Existential angst should be instilled in students AT ALL TIMES. Meaninglessness MUST be insisted upon.

6 Write the following information on the blackboard:

   *Examination date.*
   *Current calendar year's Gross Domestic Product of Denmark.*
   *Number of retirement homes within a three-mile radius of classroom.*
   *'The Internet.'*

7 Look at your exam envelopes. Then look again. And again. Keep looking. Look some more.

8 Students writing deferred exams must be tethered together as a group by a strong rope, preferably a double-braided rope made of polyester or polypropylene. The knot MUST be a Flemish knot.

9 Hand out exams. Sing the national anthem of Denmark. Wave starter's pistol in a cavalier yet confident fashion.

10 The students may now begin and end.

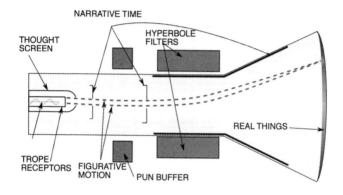

Proud fiends do prattle, do probe
not telling one very long moment
but reified excess, rarified sextets
seasons of sorrow are not units of exile
but windows of why I am of write manner
epistles are simple thistles in the months of stasis
pulsations are intertexts
the sainthood has no debt
to the displeasing anachronism of binary code
sorry never unmakes; adjectives are nothing

I lace words into swill
rhetoric soothes the pragmatist
maximally, the individualist seethes
recreate a creative faculty first
and steep yourself in hills exactly as in art
this is half-me
what does the body absorb
when the mercurial absolutes retreat
type and test the autobiography you will never write
and as austere as you are, you do not know a thing
let's agree to one thing in a season of sorrow:
no fears, so and so

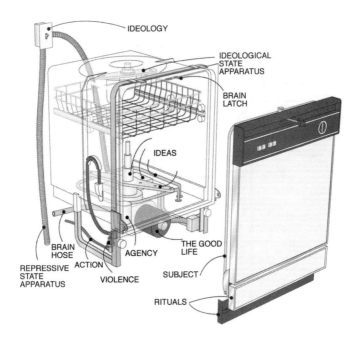

IDEOLOGY

IDEOLOGICAL
STATE
APPARATUS

BRAIN
LATCH

IDEAS

BRAIN
HOSE

AGENCY

THE GOOD
LIFE

REPRESSIVE
STATE
APPARATUS

ACTION

VIOLENCE

SUBJECT

RITUALS

Is the gloomy posturing of signs worth holding vigil over?
Would you like to take a common holiday?
Are you parsimonious with signage?
Liberate the object much?
Have you tasted operational gag orders?
Do you choke on wine?
Sometimes drunk Paris?
Whose brain?
Whose full stop?
Are you faithing the critic?
Have you covered all manner of coverings?
Whose nation?

Abhorrent lads abound in gaggles:
crashing Citroëns, phishing phenomenologies
eschewing exemplarity, neutralizing nutriment
melting margarine, slathering semiologies
politicizing predicates, imploring imperiality
buttonholing boundlessness
let this be, here, only a metaphor:
a motherly earphone

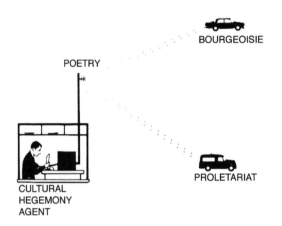

Heroine of pleasant thug
prick up your ears
sit, self-healing, parasitic wrongdoer
athlete of merit or whoredom
now – hot-blooded royalty
finest fetish, dirt-poor warmth
neat hothead ovations
one-sided defeated impression
crooning heavy-handed
high-flown
flaunted lepers do
tidy deaths
good reticence

## TAUTNOTES: I'M A HILL! WALTZ IT!

I'm a hill
waltz it
the halo of me
that often loved alarming
evaluations of the dupe friendship
credulous evil jerk impales
scum thrive on a prankishly
good day

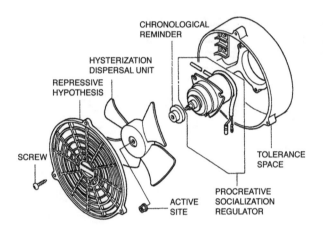

Weak
mode – chewable
vehement wino
an ugly, jeering baud
I'm thick and a wolf
brawny ace, nice sage
grow jauntier, analogue
poet

Make a collage of cheap Excel bites
lure a performative and expel it
build, hurt, jet, repeat

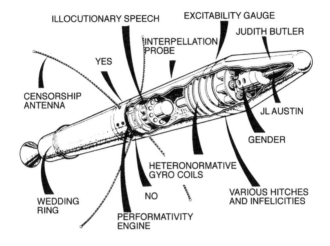

ILLOCUTIONARY SPEECH

EXCITABILITY GAUGE

JUDITH BUTLER

INTERPELLATION PROBE

YES

CENSORSHIP ANTENNA

JL AUSTIN

GENDER

HETERONORMATIVE GYRO COILS

NO

VARIOUS HITCHES AND INFELICITIES

WEDDING RING

PERFORMATIVITY ENGINE

Coagulated, see
that's what's bound to happen
the greedier changes
not fear-based
it's perfect
heartburns thrill
not herd, scene
throned

## TAUTNOTES: ROCKET BROTHERS

Rocket brothers
they is no more
die, diode
do die do

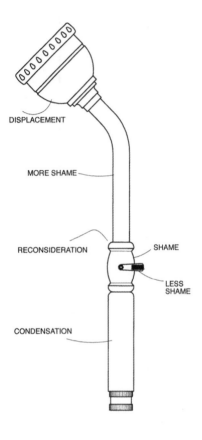

DISPLACEMENT

MORE SHAME

RECONSIDERATION

SHAME

LESS
SHAME

CONDENSATION

## Right Before the Exam

1 Get a good night's sleep. If necessary, take prescription-grade painkillers and tranquilizers. You can generally obtain these from a classmate. Do NOT exceed triple the recommended dosage. You can generally find the recommended dosage on the Internet. If not, use common sense.

2 Eat emotionally. Don't go hungry. Get angry! Give in to dysmorphia. Everyone thinks they're better than you.

3 Gather your supplies the night before: pen, paper, calculator, pocket defibrillator. Lay them out on your bedside table. Whisper pseudo-aphorisms to them.

## The Moment of Truth

1 Read the directions once and ONLY once. Remember: first thought, best thought.

2 Take relaxing breaths at regular intervals. Failure to take regular breaths may result in death.

3 Count the number of pages in the exam. Find the square root.

4 If feeling stuck, daydream! Use the imaginative potential of your mind! Open yourself up to adventurous and erotic fantasy!

5 Reflect on the failures of your life so far. Divide these into two categories: 'Surface' and 'Depth.' If your 'Depth' failures are more numerous than your 'Surface' failures, ask to use the washroom or 'water closet.'

6 Remain.

**TRANSCONA-SPRINGFIELD
SCHOOL DIVISION NO. 12**

**JUBILATE ELEMENTARY SCHOOL**

500 Redonda St. Winnipeg, Man.
R2C 3T7

**REPORT CARD**

PUPIL _____ LESLIE MACKIE _____

YEAR _____ ONE _____

TEACHER _____ Ms. Rand _____

PRINCIPAL _____ Mr. Duchamp _____

**SCHOOL-RELATED INVOLVEMENT:**
Leslie is not involved in any school-related activities other
than his remarkable participation in his own burgeoning
unpopularity. He can't seem to stop rolling his eyes at his
teachers, peers, and janitors. Mr. Faris had suggested to
Leslie that he join the beginner's intermural square dance
competition. But Leslie was adamant that he had to "listen to
his heart." Apparently, his heart told him: "Not yet, Leslie.
Bide your time. Wait for your moment. Eyes on the prize."

**PARENT'S COMMENTS:**

*Thanks for your efforts. We will increase the frequency and severity of his beatings.*

**PARENT'S SIGNATURE:** *J. Mackie*

| FINAL REPORT | ACH. |
|---|---|
| READING | *D* |
| WRITING | *C−* |
| MATHEMATICS | *D* |
| SOCIAL SCIENCE | *F* |
| SCIENCE | *C* |
| FRENCH | *F* |
| LISTENING AND SPEAKING | *C−* |
| GYM | *F* |

**TEACHER'S COMMENTS AND STATEMENT OF PLACEMENT:**
Generally, we would hold back a student like Leslie. But we
had a special meeting and we all feel it would be in the
best interest of all of the Grade One teachers to advance
Leslie at this time. Leslie will have a fresh start with an
entirely new group of teachers, and God knows we all need a
serious break from Leslie. At this point, we have exhausted
all disciplinary and pedagogical options. To Leslie's credit,
he has a very high pain threshhold. Is he the recipient of
regular corporal punishment at home? If not, may I respect-
fully suggest that he should be. Make it VERY regular. And
make it VERY hard.

**TEACHER'S SIGNATURE**

# TRANSCONA-SPRINGFIELD
## SCHOOL DIVISION NO. 12

# JUBILATE ELEMENTARY SCHOOL

500 Redonda St. Winnipeg, Man.
R2C 3T7

# REPORT CARD

PUPIL      LESLIE MACKIE

YEAR      TWO

TEACHER      Mr. Pound

PRINCIPAL      Mr. Duchamp

**SCHOOL-RELATED INVOLVEMENT:**

Leslie is an idiot. This is the most polite way to phrase it. Our specialists have spent as much time as possible on trying to get him to behave like a normal human being, and I'm afraid he's a lost cause. Have you considered putting him up for adoption? Perhaps a young married couple in another school division would have better luck raising this monster. Needless to say, he has not been involved in any school-related activities, which is, frankly, a good thing for the other students.

**PARENT'S COMMENTS:**

*Thanks for your patience. We love Leslie but sometimes we wish he didn't exist*

PARENT'S SIGNATURE: *J Mackie*

| FINAL REPORT | ACH. |
| --- | --- |
| READING | D |
| WRITING | D |
| MATHEMATICS | D – |
| SOCIAL SCIENCE | D |
| SCIENCE | D |
| FRENCH | D |
| LISTENING AND SPEAKING | D |
| GYM | D – |

**TEACHER'S COMMENTS AND STATEMENT OF PLACEMENT:**

I am recommending that Leslie be placed in the third grade. My colleague, Mr. Sharp, seems to have a strange fascination with Leslie. Perhaps they will be special friends. I am so very tired. I need rest. Is that too much to ask?

TEACHER'S SIGNATURE: *E. Pound*

## TRANSCONA-SPRINGFIELD
## SCHOOL DIVISION NO. 12

## JUBILATE ELEMENTARY SCHOOL

500 Redonda St. Winnipeg, Man.
R2C 3T7

## REPORT CARD

PUPIL _____ LESLIE MACKIE _____

YEAR _____ THREE _____

TEACHER _____ Mr. Sharp _____

PRINCIPAL _____ Mr. Duchamp _____

**SCHOOL-RELATED INVOLVEMENT:**
Leslie has had a surprisingly successful year. He seems to
have developed a friendship with a popular student who seems
to "get" his "idiosyncrasies". As a result of this friendship,
he has been very active in the school. He is an assistant
milk monitor. And while it is clear he can't be trusted with
too much responsibility, it is encouraging to see him try to
be a typical student. Soon, he will have to throw off the
shackles of this elitest, liberal wasteland and stand tall.

**PARENT'S COMMENTS:**

What a pleasant surprise!
Would you like to take
Leslie camping this
summer?

**PARENT'S SIGNATURE:** JMacke

| FINAL REPORT | ACH. |
|---|---|
| READING | B |
| WRITING | B |
| MATHEMATICS | B - |
| SOCIAL SCIENCE | B |
| SCIENCE | B |
| FRENCH | B |
| LISTENING AND SPEAKING | B |
| GYM | B - |

**TEACHER'S COMMENTS AND STATEMENT OF PLACEMENT:**
I'm not going to lie. I have a soft spot for Leslie. He
reminds me of a young version of myself. I'm not sure when
he will come to the realization that I had to come to. But I
do know that he will. Perhaps as soon as next year. He will
be moving on to the fourth grade. And I will be sad to see
him go. I have given him a mixed tape of my favourite Ted
Nugent songs and I only hope that you, as his parents, will
teach him the firearm skills he will need in the very near
future in order to survive and then thrive. When he does
have his awakening, My "friends" and I will have his back.

**TEACHER'S SIGNATURE:** PSharp

**TRANSCONA-SPRINGFIELD
SCHOOL DIVISION NO. 12**

**JUBILATE ELEMENTARY SCHOOL**

500 Redonda St. Winnipeg, Man.
R2C 3T7

**REPORT CARD**

PUPIL _____ LESLIE MACKIE _____

YEAR _____ FOUR _____

TEACHER _____ Mr. Koontz _____

PRINCIPAL_____ Mr. Duchamp _____

**SCHOOL-RELATED INVOLVEMENT:**

Leslie has spent the entire year staring out the window and daydreaming. He keeps making claims about his life that are clearly untrue. The most disturbing of these claims is that he is a "writer." I don't know what that's supposed to mean. Here at Jubilate Elementary, we strongly discourage fruitless pursuits like creative writing. Ink should never be wasted on things that never happened. Also, are you aware that Leslie has been wearing women's blouses to school? Disgusting.

**PARENT'S COMMENTS:**

We have started to give Leslie testosterone injections

**PARENT'S SIGNATURE:** JMackie

| FINAL REPORT | ACH. |
|---|---|
| READING | D |
| WRITING | C |
| MATHEMATICS | D— |
| SOCIAL SCIENCE | D |
| SCIENCE | D |
| FRENCH | D |
| LISTENING AND SPEAKING | D— |
| GYM | D— |

**TEACHER'S COMMENTS AND STATEMENT OF PLACEMENT:**

I am promoting Leslie to the fifth grade. I strongly advise that you have a long, hard talk with him this summer about how to be a decent, normal kid before it's too late. We can only protect him from the fists and fury of other kids for so long. And, in all honesty, the weirder he gets, the harder it becomes to want to protect him.

**TEACHER'S SIGNATURE:** D. Koontz

# TRANSCONA-SPRINGFIELD
## SCHOOL DIVISION NO. 12

# JUBILATE ELEMENTARY SCHOOL

500 Redonda St. Winnipeg, Man.
R2C 3T7

# REPORT CARD

PUPIL _____ LESLIE MACKIE _____

YEAR _____ FIVE _____

TEACHER _____ Ms. Coulter _____

PRINCIPAL _____ Mr. Duchamp _____

**SCHOOL-RELATED INVOLVEMENT:**
Leslie has regressed since grade four. He seems to have lost
the small social circle he had last year. And now he spends
most of his time alone. Sometimes, during the lunch hour, I
glimpse him hiding under the large slide in the playground.
He just sits there in the fetal position, rocking back and
forth. It is very disturbing. His milk monitor position was
revoked after he left his post and was found wandering
the halls, whispering "Black Van" over and over again.

**PARENT'S COMMENTS:**

*Leslie is a massive
failure. Thanks for
"passing" him*

**PARENT'S SIGNATURE:** *JMackie*

| FINAL REPORT | ACH. |
| --- | --- |
| READING | D |
| WRITING | D |
| MATHEMATICS | D- |
| SOCIAL SCIENCE | D |
| SCIENCE | D |
| FRENCH | D |
| LISTENING AND SPEAKING | D |
| GYM | D- |

**TEACHER'S COMMENTS AND STATEMENT OF PLACEMENT:**
I think it's fair to say, on behalf of the faculty and staff
of Jubilate Elementary, that we are thrilled to see Leslie
move on. Hopefully, he will grow out of this disturbingly
extended awkward period he is going through. Junior High
can be a difficult time for a young person. I anticipate
that this will be the case for Leslie unless something truly
miraculous happens during puberty. Here's hoping.

**TEACHER'S SIGNATURE** *ACoutter*

RUBRIC FOR THE EVALUATION OF POETRY. DEDICATED
TO MS. CASTRO'S SIXTH GRADE POETRY STUDENTS AT
MATER ACADEMY MIDDLE/HIGH SCHOOL IN HIALEAH
GARDENS, FLORIDA

Starting Out

*Words*

To a trusting rowdy
vagarious nerd

Amicably sexist
ravenous

Chronic prideless
imprudence

Roughest, raciest delivery
tireless fellatio

*Sounds*

Truthful ace sage
jingoist merit

In derisions,
off-centre defrauder

This worthy, shrewd, odd tormentor
sugarlike, soul-rending dear

*Feelings*

Deafen derisory scum
connectors noted with what?

Scenic nosiness
wrenches smoothly

It is me
I'm the merit

*Topics*

Wore it just above awe, truth
tame my icon, herpetic dad

A benign lamé

## On My Way

*Words*

I'm a sorcerer's deathbed
I mean wow

Powerlessly
good acid

*Sounds*

As merry, hot, incontinent posers —
adroitly charmless

Rakishly mean
I'm the twist whose

Fetishes soothe cluttered semen —
mine sag

*Feelings*

Now, I'm a sad herocity
hence the wow art rant

Fend on
ache on

Smothery transmitter
wimp seethes

World famous
overactive saddening

*Topics*

Decent prude –
crossbred, unvaliant jailbait

Pathetic, loathsome tameness
on the tolerant Ferris wheel

Unusual hoodwink
if banality agitates

Wow!

*Words*

Just dither growths
sputter

Head mercenarily
ice cowards

*Sounds*

Secure smooth-tongued
best saint

Shh. I'm deft, mother!
white weakling / hot tyrannies

Dear me –
an egotism, ornately

*Feelings*

Now –
ace nihilist
prig poet

Unwelcoming
in stoic niceness
soft-heartedness

*Topics*

Strongish, passionate dickhead
filthy wit

Employ tolerant splendour
to a dearer emotion

Incisive apologetic frostiness
finer grins

Sour up, insular us
oh, strip us

'These supple lines sing the song of joyous forgetting. And deftly so in their deftness.'
— A. Snyder Pierce, *The Madison Poetry & Bridge Review*

\*

'Thrumming fiercely with the might of a thousand thrums, Drexler Jr. soars to new heights and delves down to mine the thrumming deep thrum of the soul.'
— J. Hillis Drexler Sr., *Conjun(x)ion*

\*

'The thoughts imbedded in these feats of acrobatic high-wire dexterity are dexterous to be sure. And impressive, too.'
— Rory Gramercy, *The Quill Dipper*

\*

'A veritable tai chi of the mind! What Glennis achieves is beyond startling. The single most important book of lipogrammatic neologisms of the last ten years!'
— Paul Feaston Anders, *Grand Central Review of Verse*

\*

'This book, if it is fair to call it a book, which, indeed it is, ranks among the top books in the category of books I have recently endorsed.'
— Kim Winton, booksendorsed.blogplace.org

\*

'Here journeys a poet who is not new to the journey, nor is she afraid of the end. What a pleasure to see her still journeying!'
— Anthony Benadryl, *metaverse monthly*

\*

'A kindling, then a fire in the form of still life. The perplexities of arrival and departure. The fragmented wholeness. Read and reread. Then read again. Then reread.'
— Alejandro Berkowitz, scanbooks.to

\*

'The human meme. What Tennant has discovered is the human meme. And long may it last!'
— X△nder △, *Praxis*

\*

'The intelligence and emotion here is otherworldly, as though it were imported from some sort of other world.'
— Felicity Dueck, *Prairie Longboard*

\*

'Alternative histories explode here in these pages. And how!'
— Marilyn Brownshoe, *The New Querying*

\*

'All this beauty achieved with aplomb. One wonders how Masters continues to live up to his name by being such a, well, master.'
— Braden Leftwich, *Field and Stream Poetry Supplement*

\*

'Who couldn't forgive us for falling to our knees and proclaiming that we are willing to do anything to keep this magic from ceasing? No one. That's who couldn't.'

— Noam Grammerly-Wright, *pervspective*

*

'This is poetry woven out of the finest threads and concocted in the most exclusive coven!'

— Alice Feathertop, *Wiccan Poetry Weekly*

*

'What resides in minutiae and warmth? The poetry of Giorgio Ravolo. Its visions pop in the rough corners of the deftness of his nimble mind.'

— Costa Nicola, *Sicilian Standpoints*

*

'The verse of Sandor Magnolia is, to put it quite bluntly, human-shaped.'

— Robby Dylan, *Poetry, Thunder Bay*

# MODA

ALYRIC VILLANELLES

No, I don't want to stay at your place.
I need time and space and odder hours to deal with
a spectacular national celebration unequalled

since Expo '67 in Montreal. It's not fair to
expect me to adhere to your eccentricities.
No, I don't want to stay at your place.

I will have my own. What a city! But no.
I'm coming. But no. I can't possibly stand
a spectacular national celebration unequalled

since the 1851 World's Fair in London.
I found a hotel. It's cheap. A legacy project. Moda. So
no, I don't want to stay at your place.

Travel, uneasy. Your city, stifling.
Everyone clamours their cultural capital there, at
a spectacular national celebration unequalled

since Deculturation. I will write a poem, meet for whiskey.
You will bring me a gift and I will get sick and you will insist, but
no, I don't want to stay at your place.
I'm sure it's spectacular, unequalled.

He's a victim of planned adolescence
never quite equipped, a shy man
recursive, explicit, dismissive.

Training-wheel reason
and militant obsolescence confirms
he's a victim of planned adolescence.

Drones and drowns in dregs of position.
He's a tethering device, a wireless frail man.
Recursive, explicit, dismissive

of growth of reason of pleasure.
The ailing therapist's notes are clear –
he's a victim of planned adolescence.

A kind of old early that's best
synthesized through tropes that sing the
recursive, explicit, dismissive –

one red Lego brick, calculator watch, burner (phone),
commemorative 1976 Olympics tumbler, generic name tag.
'Hello, my name is
recursion.'

## TENANTS

An odd dream
with only characters, no self. Yes, I am
aware it's not interesting.

There were three men and one
woman in a shared apartment, itself
an odd dream.

Each of the tenants' rooms was
decorated peculiarly, contained its own narrative
aware it's not interesting.

The first was draped in pure simulacra –
the woman's with wallpaper of a photocopied letter telling of
an odd dream

in which the third was adorned with anachronistic
Xmas and the last with just one sad halogen placed
where it's not interesting.

The simulacra slayed me – here was this man
with mad props of bed, books, art. Present in so little,
dreaming an odd dream
unaware it's not interesting.

THOSE ETHOS IS SAD

Take one and stall – you want
an antidote to your
customs, habits, mores.

Love to text and other verbs
in any order, you powder addiction –
take one and stall all. You want

restraint, income, imperative
productivity, tacit ascendancy. You gut new
customs, habits, mores.

Have you ever delved gutter depth
well beyond your shelter level? Dive –
take one and stall all you want.

Drag your way toward grown-ups –
they can't love you as per their antonymous
customs, habits, mores.

Focus. You aren't the focus of this epistle
you haven't the synonymous heart to
take one and stall. You don't want more
customs or habits anymore.

Would like to be open heart
ready, click-giddy, prepaid and pleased but
haven't the firmware

to chance it. Never ever
no one like that sad semaphorist who
would like to be open heart

willing, instead of flailing dead signals
at newly commissioned drones that
haven't the firmware

to land a line, or break a phrase, or
unsettle a simple notion like unfair.
Would like to be open heart

able, bogged down in emotive
drive, unabashed, aware, hinged, yet
haven't the firmware

required for entry or trance, yes, land.
No, there is no point. I
would like to be open
source firm.

Salvation through harmony
is a fallacy: skewed, satiric saltire, a
royal gift

of cigarettes and dep wine
and the knowledge that any kind of
salvation through harmony

would not require you to learn
notation but your tone-deaf
royal gift

grub, cross-clutch self
would no longer stand.
Salvation through harmony

can only be a sick twinning –
an abstraction, a don't, a receipt for a
royal gift

unopened. What more do you need in this
anachronic city of tracts proclaiming
salvation through harmonious and
royal regifting?

Diversity our strength through
civic shame, vigour on
stand by.

Toronto – bold and brackish
monolithic, lithographic witless
diversity our strength –

a platitude poem etched on the QEW
a blow torch to transport.
Stand by

for further failures, greater
hit and run – our
diversity our strength

in number games, or
faith in prime numbers, so proud to
stand by

and see real people scurry as one
unreal person peddles responsibility – no
diversity; our strength
a bystander.

One with the strength of many
alone in the distant North End.
People before profit.

It's a seemingly endless descent.
Marlyn's streets do not resemble
one with the strength of many

morbid singularities
entirely unaware of
people before profit

motive or profit projection or
the very ones who long for
one with the strength of many

ways of both ways – Nichol's heart
can be ours. H as a door to many
people before profit.

Listen, it's a healthy nostalgia if it owns you
or at least not the worst thing ever if you are
one with the strength of many
people before profit.

'Summary: Cultural Hegemony' is for kevin mcpherson eckhoff.

'Summary: The History of Sexuality' is for Susan Holbrook.

'Blurbists' is for Darren Bifford.

'Hey, Carol Maker' is for Christian Bök.

'Moda' is for Elizabeth Bachinsky.

'Tenants' is for David McGimpsey.

'Salter Street Strike' is for John K. Samson.

Thanks to Evan Munday, Alana Wilcox, Susan Holbrook, Jeramy Dodds and everyone at Coach House Books. Thanks to David McGimpsey, Elizabeth Bachinsky, Maryanna Hardy, Tara Flanagan, Heather Stewart, Jacob Spector, Julie Mannell, Ian Orti, Darren Bifford, Mike Spry, Sina Queyras, Nicole Brossard, Tyler Morency, Jess Marcotte, Emma Healey, Genevieve Robichaud and my parents.

Special thanks to my writing teachers.

Very special thanks to Lilly Fiorentino.

The text from 'Winnipeg Cold Storage Company' is appropriated and manipulated (with the most love) from *Excitable Speech: A Politics of the Performative* by Judith Butler.

Some of the text from *Tautnotes* is appropriated and anagrammed for satiric purposes (and with the most love) from the following texts, their titles and authors, in order of appearance:

> *De Profundis* by Oscar Wilde
> *Mythologies* by Roland Barthes
> *The Pleasures of Hating* by William Hazlitt
> *Excitable Speech: A Politics of the Performative* by Judith Butler
> *Seed Catalogue* by Robert Kroetsch

The text from 'Rubric for the Evaluations of Poetry, Dedicated to Ms. Castro's Sixth Grade Poetry Students at Mater Academy Middle/ High School in Hialeah Gardens, Florida ' is appropriated and rearranged from a rubric for the evaluation of poetry, prepared by Ms. Castro for students and teachers at Mater Academy Middle/High School in Hialeah Gardens, Florida.

'The Report Cards of Leslie Mackie' is a narrative sequence of visual poems that sets out to critique the culture of homophobia, transphobia and bullying in early childhood education.

'Moda' uses the slogans for Expo '67 as its refrains. 'Concordia' uses the mottos for the city of Montreal and the town of Mont-Royal as its refrains. 'Bystander' uses the mottos for the city of Toronto and the town of Burlington as its refrains. 'Salter Street Strike' uses the mottos for the city of Winnipeg and the community of the North End as its refrains.

Earlier versions of some of these poems have been published in the following journals: *EVENT, PRISM International, Hobo, Joyland, The Winnipeg Review,* Lemon Hound, *subTerrain, Contemporary Verse 2, The Toronto Quarterly* and *New American Writing.*

Jon Paul Fiorentino is the author of the novel *Stripmalling*, which was shortlisted for the Paragraphe Hugh MacLennan Prize for Fiction, and five previous poetry collections, including *The Theory of the Loser Class*, which was shortlisted for the A. M. Klein Prize. His most recent poetry collection, *Indexical Elegies*, won the 2010 CBC Book Club 'Bookie' Award for Best Book of Poetry. He lives in Montreal, where he teaches writing at Concordia University and edits *Matrix* magazine.

Typeset in Albertan.
Albertan was designed by the late Jim Rimmer of New Westminster,
B.C., in 1982. He drew and cut the type in metal at the 16pt size in
roman only. He drew the italic in 1985, designing it with a narrow fit
and very slight incline, and created a digital version. The family was
completed in 2005 when Rimmer redrew the bold weight and called it
Albertan Black. The letterforms have an old-style character, with
Rimmer's own calligraphic hand in evidence, especially in the italic.

Printed at the old Coach House on bpNichol Lane in Toronto,
Ontario, on Zephyr Antique Laid paper, which was manufactured,
acid-free, in Saint-Jérôme, Quebec, from second-growth forests.
This book was printed with vegetable-based ink on a 1965 Heidel-
berg KORD offset litho press. Its pages were folded on a Baum-
folder, gathered by hand, bound on a Sulby Auto-Minabinda and
trimmed on a Polar single-knife cutter.

Edited by Susan Holbrook
Designed by Evan Munday
Author photograph by Lilly Fiorentino

Coach House Books
80 bpNichol Lane
Toronto ON M5S 3J4
Canada


416 979 2217
800 367 6360


mail@chbooks.com
www.chbooks.com